Colors

PLAY BAC
PUBLISHING

More.Brain.Power

Walking through the pages of this book, curious young readers will discover nature's many colors.

Those who take a closer look will find a thousand shades, because whether is it forest, olive, or apple, no green is the same!

Nature changes with the seasons and so do colors. At the beach, on the ground, or in the sky, they come in every shade imaginable. So to see every color in nature's rainbow, let's look at the world around us and keep our eyes open.

After all, nature is an excellent teacher!

canary

sunflower

Yellow

sponge

grapefruit

lemon
yellow

4

Sunflower, lemon,
Flowers and fruits;
Canary, chick, and duckling,
All in yellow suits!

lemon

duckling

chick

daffodil

golden
yellow

mustard
yellow

Yellow

bananas

an ear of corn

toucan

The toucan's beak is golden-yellow,
Corn and bananas are more mellow;
They are a lighter yellow!

Red is red, dark or light.
On little bugs or on flowers,
Red is always bright.

gerbera

ladybug

firebugs

Red

poppy

Red

Ripe red berries
Plucked from the tree
Bright red coral
Under the sea

cherries

coral

tomato

goldfish

red currants

strawberry

red coral

fire engine red

tomato red

From Red to Green

Red Chief

Royal Gala

Golden Russet

Red, golden, yellow and green; apples to be eaten, not just seen!

Golden Delicious

Granny Smith

leaf

frog

lizard

ivy

Green

Frogs and insects have it made!
Hiding in grass and clover,
the same green shade.

grass

grasshopper

clover

caterpillar

lettuce

Green

So much to choose from, all in green,

olives

zucchini

cucumber
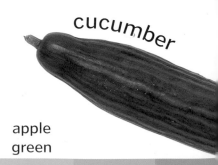

leaf green

apple
green

salad, side-dish, or green bean!

green beans

peas

cabbage

artichoke

spinach

sea green

forest green

olive green

leaf

From Green to Brown

Green, yellow, orange, brown...
When fall arrives, they all fall down!

Brown

fox

hen

*What do you think
this fox can see?*

mushroom

pinecone

horse chestnut

sweet chestnut

soil

tree bark

squirrel

A hen, a squirrel,
the bark of a tree.

slug

acorn

peanuts

Tan

A bit of brown,
plenty of white,
Mix them together;
Tan looks right!

turtledove

Labrador

walnut

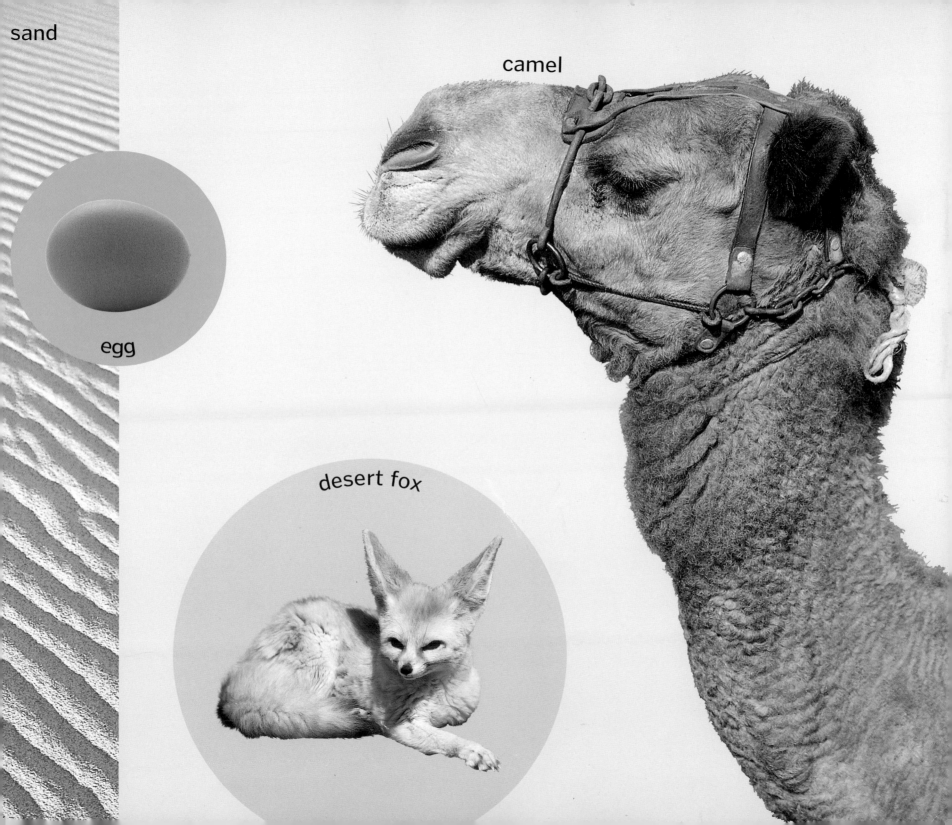

sand

egg

camel

desert fox

Blue

turquoise blue

navy blue

midnight blue

parrot
feathers

macaw

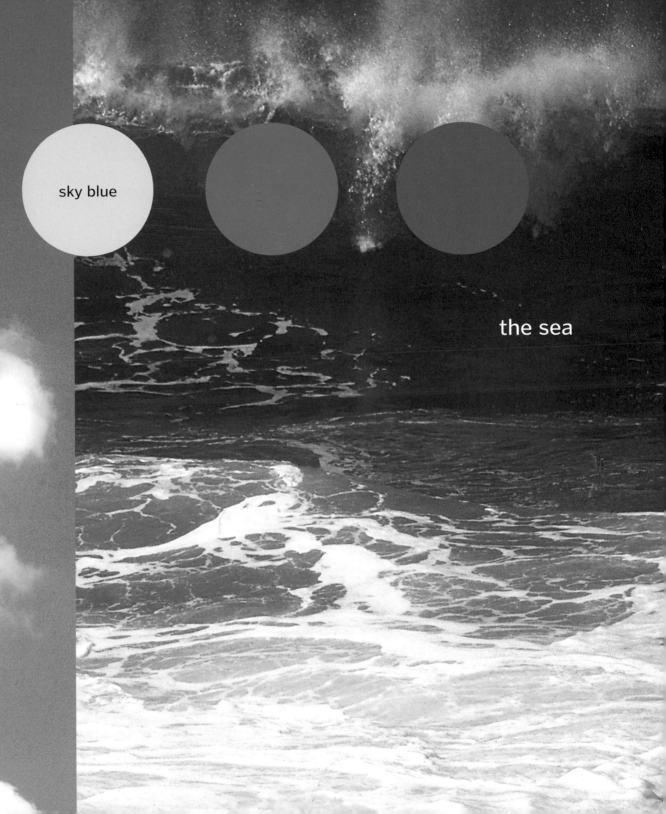

sky blue

the sea

The sea, the sky,
the feathers that fly,
They're all blue,
and that will do!

the sky

From Blue to Orange

the sky

Blue sky by day, then orange comes out to play!

carrots

apricot

cantaloupe

orange

Orange is the brightest of all,
from the biggest pumpkin to the small.

clementine

pumpkin

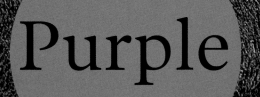

Purple

field of lavender

Eggplant peels and lavender fields
Purple is really real!

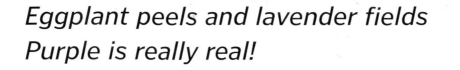

blueberry

eggplant

periwinkle

Purple

iris

eggplant

plum

lilac

lilac

Pansy, pansy, what do you see?
Vivid violets and a lilac tree!

pansy

violets

Transparent

You can see through it!
It's apparent!
No, it's transparent!
It doesn't have a color!
It's absent!
No, it's translucent!

drop of water

air bubbles

leaf

shrimp

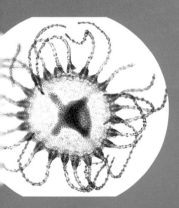

jellyfish

Translucent

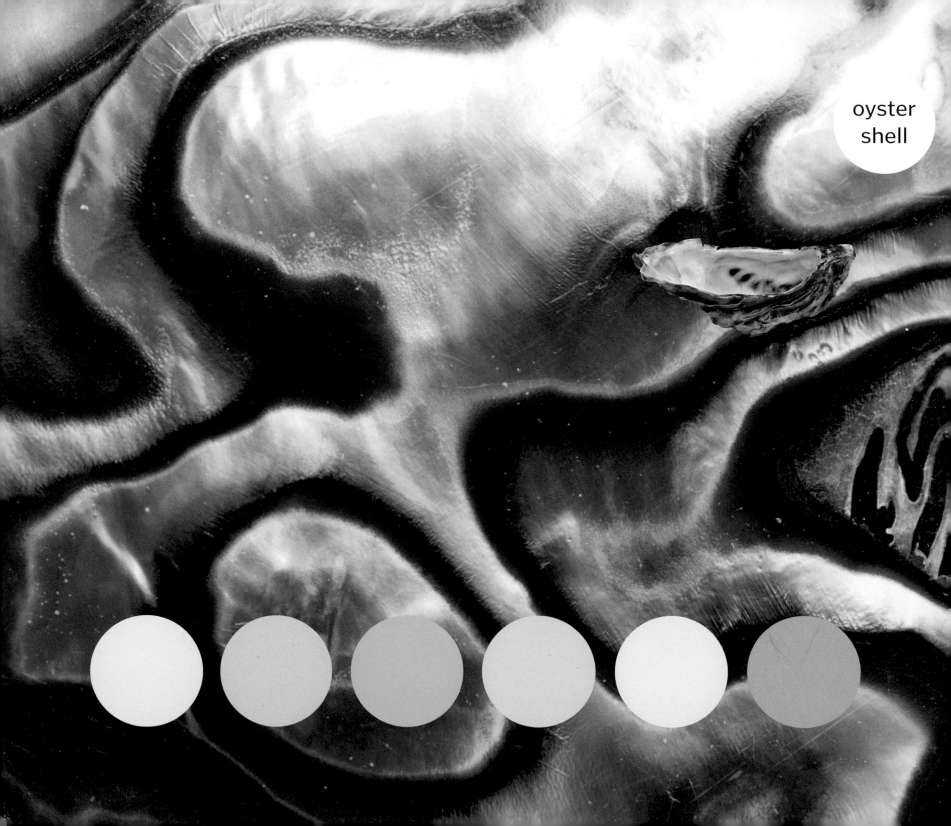

oyster
shell

Iridescent, pearly

pearl

shell

The pearly shell and the iridescent pearl are so lucky: they shine and change colour in the sun.

Pink

pink flamingo

raspberry pink

fuchsia

baby pink

What does this flamingo think? He is the champion of all shades of pink!

raspberries

cherry blossoms

piglet

radish

*What do you think this
pig would like to try?
Berries, flowers,
and radishes, oh, my!*

Gray

heron

What color are these pebbles?
Not quite black!
Not quite white!

pebbles

pearl gray

mouse gray

charcoal gray

elephant

mouse

What do mouse and elephant share?
Their gray color, their friendly stare.

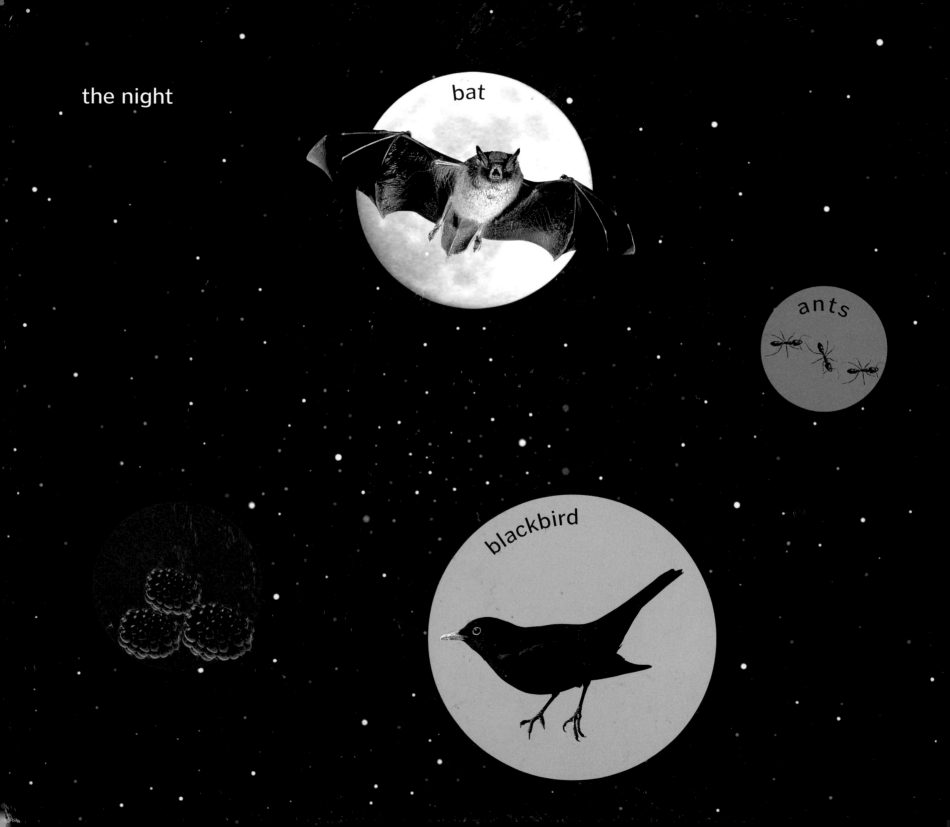

the night

bat

ants

blackbird

Black

Light black? Take that back.
Dark black?
You can't say that.
Black is black,
and that is that!

cat

White

swan

How do they keep their feathers so bright?

goose

White

snow

*Flowers as beautiful as snow,
Pretty and white and lovely to grow!*

edelweiss

daisy

dove

calla lily

ice

lily

The zebra likes his stripes the best.
He's more impressive than the rest!

dalmatian

magpie

Black and White

marble

zebra

emperor penguin

egg

Two-
tone

coconut

onion

*The egg, the coconut, and the onion
all have something to hide:
a second color hidden inside!*

Multicolor

butterfly

tulip

1, 2, 3, go!
The butterflies are not so slow
to find their matching flowers!

Multicolor

fish

Under the sea
Take a chance
Come to the colorful
Coral reef dance!

coral

Photography credits:
Meaning of the letters:
h : top ; b : bottom ; d : right ; g : left : c : center.

ASK IMAGES : Bartolucci E. : 47g, 53d.

BIOS : Bach J.-C. : 40g ; Barbelette E. : 20bd ; Bertani T. : 33hd ; Bolton M. : 31bg ; Cahez F. : 48hd ; Cavignaux P.: 24g ; Collection Leber : 20bcg ; Cox D./OSF : 49bd ; Da Cunha T. : 8c ; Denis-Huot M. & C. : 41d, 15bd ; Douillet J. : 17hc, 32 & 33 ; Feve F. : 33b ; Gilson F. : 14bd ; Grospas J.-Y. : 14hd, 46hd ; Gunther M. : 4hg, 18 & 19 ; Halleux D.: 4 & 5 ; Klein-Hubert : 20hg, 22bg, 24d, 25d ; Le Fèvre M. : 34cg ; Lemoigne J.-L. : 20bg ; Lenain H. : 32g ; Lopez G.: 42bc ; Lundberg P. : 44 & 45 ; Malausa J.-C. : 15g ; Marquez F. : 38 ; Mayet J. : 8bd ; Petit T. : 23bc ; Prévot J.M : 14c, 46bg ; Sement D. : 48 & 49 ; Stoerckle T. : 42h ; Vidal F. : 39bc ; Ziegler J.-L. & F. : 9.

COLIBRI : Lavergne J.-Y. : 4bg ; Testu C. : 10hd, 55bg.

GETTY : Biodisc : 35g ; Bracegirdle J. : 21d ; China Tourism Press : 10 & 11b ; Darrell Gulin : 36 ; Davies & Starr : 37g ; Elsdale B. : 20cd ; GSO Images : 36hg ; Kelly M. : 35d ; Knowles J. : 34g ; Lawrence J. : 2 ; Travelpix Ltd : cover and spine/h.

HACHETTE PHOTOS : Desmier X./RAPHO : 34c.

PHONE : Balanca E. : 22hd ; Grenet-Soumillard : 15hd, 21bg ; Labat J.-M. & Rocher P. : 41g.

PHOTONONSTOP : Mauritius : 34d.

SUNSET : FLPA : 7, cover/c.

Marc Schwarz : 6 & 7b, 6g, 10g, 11d, 11hg, 12 & 13, 16 & 17b, 16 & 17h, 16c, 16g, 17bc, 17hd, 20bcd, 21bc, 23hg, 28bg, 28hg, 29b, 29hd, 31c, 39g, front cover/bc and spine/c, 50 & 51, 50g.

Acknowledgments:
Play Bac Publishing wishes to thank all the teachers, mothers, and children who have helped develop the eyelike series.

SPECIAL THANKS to: Frédéric Michaud, Claire Despine, Anne Burrus, Beryl Motte, Munira Al-Khalili, Elizabeth Van Houten and Paula Manzanero.

All the books in the Play Bac series have been tested by families and teachers and edited and proofread by professionals in the field.

ISBN-13 : 978-1-60214-019-6

Play Bac Publishing USA, Inc.
225 Varick Street, New York, NY 10014-4381

Printed in Singapore by TWP

Distributed by Black Dog & Leventhal Publishers, Inc.
151 West 19th Street, New York, NY 10011

First printing, September 2007

In the same series: